ADVERSARIAL ATTACKS AND DEFENSES: EXPLORING FGSM AND PGD

Hacking AI

WILLIAM J. LAWRENCE

Adversarial Attacks and Defenses: Exploring FGSM and PGD

By
William J. Lawrence

Table of Contents

Foreword

In the rapidly evolving landscape of artificial intelligence and machine learning, the pursuit of robustness and security has emerged as a paramount concern. As algorithms and models become increasingly integrated into our daily lives, their vulnerability to adversarial attacks has become more evident. In this book, "Adversarial Attacks and Defenses: Exploring FGSM and PGD," we embark on a profound exploration of two fundamental techniques in the realm of adversarial machine learning: the Fast Gradient Sign Method (FGSM) and the Projected Gradient Descent (PGD) method.

In the world of AI and deep learning, we've witnessed remarkable progress in tasks such as image recognition, natural language processing, and autonomous decision-making. Yet, as these systems have grown in complexity and capability, they've also become susceptible to subtle and malicious manipulations. Adversarial attacks, characterized by carefully crafted perturbations to input data, have the potential to deceive, mislead, and compromise the integrity of AI systems. In response, researchers and practitioners have been driven to develop robust defenses that can withstand these adversarial assaults.

This book, authored by experts in the field, serves as a beacon in the quest for understanding the dynamics of adversarial attacks and defenses. The authors meticulously delve into the inner workings of FGSM and PGD, two cornerstones in the domain of adversarial machine learning. With clarity and depth, they explore the theoretical foundations, practical implementations, and real-world implications of these techniques.

FGSM, renowned for its simplicity and effectiveness, and PGD, celebrated for its robustness, are at the forefront of the battle between attackers and defenders in the AI arena. As you traverse the pages of this book, you'll gain invaluable insights into the mechanisms behind these methods, their strengths, limitations, and their applicability in various domains.

Moreover, the authors take a holistic approach, not only elucidating the strategies of attackers and defenders but also shedding light on the broader ethical and societal dimensions of adversarial machine learning. The importance of responsible AI, transparency, and fairness is underscored, emphasizing that the pursuit of security should always be aligned with our collective commitment to ethical and responsible AI development.

"Adversarial Attacks and Defenses: Exploring FGSM and PGD" is an essential resource for researchers, practitioners, students, and anyone intrigued by the intricate dance between adversarial forces in the world of AI. As we navigate the complex intersection of AI and security, this book equips us with the knowledge and tools necessary to confront adversarial challenges head-on, fortifying our AI systems and advancing the cause of trustworthy and resilient artificial intelligence.

I commend the authors for their dedication to shedding light on this critical aspect of AI, and I am confident that this book will be a guiding compass for those who seek to understand, defend against, and ultimately overcome adversarial attacks in the ever-evolving field of machine learning.

William J. Lawrence
Sr. Data Engineering SME

Part I: Introduction to Adversarial Attacks

Chapter 1: Introduction to Adversarial Machine Learning

1.1 What is Adversarial Machine Learning?

Adversarial machine learning is a research field that explores the vulnerabilities of machine learning models, particularly neural networks, to adversarial inputs. These inputs are intentionally crafted to deceive the model into making incorrect predictions or classifications. The study of adversarial machine learning involves understanding these vulnerabilities, developing attack methods to exploit them, and designing robust defenses to protect against such attacks.

1.2 The Importance of Studying Adversarial Attacks

As machine learning models become increasingly integrated into various applications, ranging from facial recognition systems to autonomous vehicles, their security and reliability become critical. Adversarial attacks pose a significant threat to the integrity of these systems, potentially causing catastrophic failures or revealing sensitive information. Understanding the nature of these attacks and how to defend against them is crucial for ensuring the safety and privacy of users and systems that rely on machine learning.

1.3 Scope of the Book

This book aims to provide a comprehensive understanding of two prominent adversarial attack methods, the Fast Gradient Sign Method (FGSM) and Projected Gradient Descent (PGD), along with the associated defense strategies. We will explore the theoretical foundations of these attack methods, their algorithmic details, and their practical applications in a variety of settings. Additionally, we will investigate the strengths and weaknesses of each method, compare their performance, and discuss how they can be mitigated using different defense techniques.

By the end of this book, readers should have a solid grasp of the FGSM and PGD attack methods, as well as an understanding of the broader field of adversarial machine learning. The knowledge gained will enable them to assess the security of their own machine learning systems and make informed decisions about how to protect them against adversarial attacks.

In the following chapters, we will delve deeper into the world of adversarial machine learning, starting with an overview of adversarial attacks on neural networks, the creation of adversarial examples, and the motivations and applications of these attacks.

Chapter 2: Adversarial Attacks on Neural Networks

2.1 Overview of Adversarial Attacks

An adversarial attack aims to manipulate the input of a neural network, causing it to produce an incorrect output. The manipulated input, called an adversarial example, is created by applying small perturbations to the original input. These perturbations are designed to be imperceptible to humans but can cause the model to misclassify the input or produce other unintended behaviors.

Adversarial attacks can be categorized into two types: white-box and black-box attacks. In white-box attacks, the attacker has complete knowledge of the model's architecture, parameters, and training data. This knowledge allows the attacker to craft adversarial examples that are more likely to be successful. In black-box attacks, the attacker has limited or no knowledge of the model's internal workings, relying instead on probing the model with inputs and observing its outputs to create adversarial examples.

2.2 Adversarial Examples

Adversarial examples are inputs that have been intentionally modified to mislead a machine learning model. These examples often appear visually indistinguishable from the original inputs to humans but can cause the model to produce drastically different outputs. The key property of adversarial examples is that they exploit the model's vulnerabilities to induce incorrect predictions or classifications.

There are several ways to generate adversarial examples, such as gradient-based methods, optimization-based methods, and evolutionary algorithms. This book will focus on two gradient-based methods: the Fast Gradient Sign Method (FGSM) and Projected Gradient Descent (PGD).

2.3 Motivations and Applications of Adversarial Attacks

Understanding and developing adversarial attacks can have several practical applications:

Security: Adversarial attacks can expose vulnerabilities in machine learning systems, enabling researchers and developers to identify potential weaknesses and develop more robust models.
Privacy: Adversarial attacks can be used to prevent unwanted surveillance or data collection by machine learning models, such as those used in facial recognition systems.
Model Interpretability: Studying adversarial attacks can provide insights into the inner workings of neural networks, helping researchers better understand the decision-making process of these models.

Robustness Evaluation: Adversarial attacks can be employed as a benchmark to test the robustness of machine learning models, enabling developers to compare different models and choose the most secure option. In the next chapter, we will introduce the Fast Gradient Sign Method (FGSM), one of the most widely used adversarial attack techniques. We will discuss its algorithm, formulation, and the various types of attacks that can be executed using FGSM.

Chapter 3: Fast Gradient Sign Method (FGSM)

3.1 Introduction to Fast Gradient Sign Method

The Fast Gradient Sign Method (FGSM) is a simple yet effective adversarial attack technique introduced by Ian J. Goodfellow et al. in 2014. It is a gradient-based method that generates adversarial examples by adding small perturbations to the original input. These perturbations are calculated using the gradient of the loss function with respect to the input. FGSM is computationally efficient, making it an appealing choice for generating adversarial examples.

3.2 FGSM Algorithm and Formulation

The FGSM algorithm can be summarized in the following steps:

Compute the gradient of the loss function with respect to the input.
Calculate the perturbation by taking the sign of the gradient and multiplying it by a small constant, epsilon (ε).
Add the perturbation to the original input to generate the adversarial example.
Mathematically, the FGSM algorithm can be expressed as:

$$x\_adv = x + \varepsilon * sign(\nabla x\ J(x, y\_true))$$

where:

x_adv is the adversarial example
x is the original input
ε is a small constant determining the magnitude of the perturbation

sign(∇x J(x, y_true)) is the sign of the gradient of the loss function J(x, y_true) with respect to the input x

3.3 Targeted and Untargeted Attacks with FGSM

FGSM can be used to perform both targeted and untargeted attacks. In an untargeted attack, the goal is to cause the model to misclassify the input without any specific target class. This can be achieved by simply following the FGSM algorithm as described above.

In a targeted attack, the goal is to cause the model to classify the input as a specific target class. To perform a targeted FGSM attack, the algorithm can be modified by computing the gradient of the loss function with respect to the input for the target class instead of the true class. This can be expressed as:

x_adv = x - ε * sign(∇x J(x, y_target))

where y_target is the desired target class.

3.4 Limitations of FGSM

FGSM has some limitations:

The choice of epsilon (ε) affects the success of the attack. If ε is too small, the perturbation may not be sufficient to cause misclassification. If ε is too large, the perturbation may become perceptible to humans.
FGSM is a single-step attack, meaning it does not iteratively refine the adversarial example. This can result in less effective adversarial examples compared to other iterative attack methods, such as Projected Gradient Descent (PGD).

3.5 FGSM-based Attack Variants

Several attack variants have been developed based on the original FGSM algorithm. Some of these include:

Basic Iterative Method (BIM): This method applies FGSM iteratively with a small step size, refining the adversarial example at each iteration.
Momentum Iterative FGSM (MI-FGSM): This variant incorporates momentum into the iterative FGSM algorithm to stabilize the update process and improve the success rate of the attack.

In the next chapter, we will introduce Projected Gradient Descent (PGD), another popular adversarial attack technique. We will discuss its algorithm, formulation, and the types of attacks that can be executed using PGD.

Chapter 4: Projected Gradient Descent (PGD)

4.1 Introduction to Projected Gradient Descent

Projected Gradient Descent (PGD) is a more advanced adversarial attack technique that is based on the iterative application of the Fast Gradient Sign Method (FGSM). It was introduced by Madry et al. in 2017 as a means of generating stronger adversarial examples. PGD is widely regarded as a more effective attack method than FGSM, primarily because it iteratively refines the adversarial example and searches for an optimal perturbation within a specified constraint.

4.2 PGD Algorithm and Formulation

The PGD algorithm can be summarized in the following steps:

Initialize the adversarial example as the original input.
For a given number of iterations, perform the following steps:
a. Compute the gradient of the loss function with respect to the adversarial example.
b. Calculate the perturbation by taking the sign of the gradient and multiplying it by a step size, alpha (α).
c. Update the adversarial example by adding the perturbation.
d. Project the adversarial example back into the valid input space to ensure the perturbation is within the allowed constraints.
Return the final adversarial example.
Mathematically, the PGD algorithm can be expressed as:

$$x\_adv^{(t+1)} = P(x\_adv^{(t)} + \alpha * sign(\nabla x\_adv\ J(x\_adv^{(t)}, y\_true)))$$

where:

$x\_adv^{(t)}$ is the adversarial example at iteration t
P is the projection function that constrains the perturbation to the valid input space
α is the step size

sign(∇x_adv J(x_adv^(t), y_true)) is the sign of the gradient of the loss function J(x_adv^(t), y_true) with respect to the adversarial example x_adv^(t)

4.3 Targeted and Untargeted Attacks with PGD

Similar to FGSM, PGD can be used to perform both targeted and untargeted attacks. In an untargeted attack, the goal is to cause the model to misclassify the input without any specific target class. This can be achieved by simply following the PGD algorithm as described above.

In a targeted attack, the goal is to cause the model to classify the input as a specific target class. To perform a targeted PGD attack, the algorithm can be modified by computing the gradient of the loss function with respect to the adversarial example for the target class instead of the true class. This can be expressed as:

x_adv^(t+1) = P(x_adv^(t) - α * sign(∇x_adv J(x_adv^(t), y_target)))

where y_target is the desired target class.

4.4 Limitations of PGD

Although PGD is a more effective attack method than FGSM, it still has some limitations:

PGD requires more computational resources due to its iterative nature, which can make it slower compared to single-step attacks like FGSM.
The choice of step size (α) and the number of iterations can significantly affect the success of the attack. Choosing appropriate values for these parameters can be challenging.

4.5 PGD-based Attack Variants

Several attack variants have been developed based on the original PGD algorithm, some of which include:

Carlini & Wagner (C&W) Attack: This attack minimizes a custom objective function using an optimization algorithm and can generate adversarial examples with smaller perturbations than PGD.

DeepFool: This method iteratively linearizes the classifier and computes the minimum perturbation required to cross the decision boundary, resulting in an efficient and effective attack.

Chapter 5: Comparing FGSM and PGD

5.1 FGSM vs. PGD: Strengths and Weaknesses

Fast Gradient Sign Method (FGSM) and Projected Gradient Descent (PGD) are both popular adversarial attack techniques used for generating adversarial examples. However, they have distinct characteristics, strengths, and weaknesses.

Strengths and Weaknesses of FGSM:

Strength: FGSM is computationally efficient and easy to implement, as it only requires a single gradient computation.
Weakness: FGSM does not search for an optimal perturbation, which can result in weaker attacks that are easier to defend against.
Strengths and Weaknesses of PGD:

Strength: PGD is more effective than FGSM in generating stronger adversarial examples due to its iterative nature, which refines the perturbation at each step.
Weakness: PGD can be computationally expensive and slower than FGSM, especially when using a large number of iterations.
5.2 Evaluating FGSM and PGD Attacks

To evaluate the effectiveness of FGSM and PGD attacks, several metrics can be considered, including:

Success Rate: The percentage of adversarial examples that successfully cause the model to produce incorrect predictions.
Average Perturbation: The average magnitude of perturbations applied to generate the adversarial examples. Smaller perturbations are generally preferred, as they are less noticeable to humans and more likely to be within the valid input space.
Time Complexity: The computational cost and time required to generate adversarial examples. Faster attacks are more desirable for real-time applications.
5.3 Transferability of Adversarial Examples

Transferability refers to the ability of adversarial examples generated for one model to cause misclassification in another model, even if the second model has a different architecture or has been trained on different data. This property is particularly important in black-box attack scenarios, where the attacker does not have access to the target model's architecture or parameters.

In general, adversarial examples generated by PGD are more transferable than those generated by FGSM. The iterative nature of PGD allows it to find perturbations that are more likely to generalize across different models. This makes PGD-based attacks more suitable for black-box scenarios, where the attacker may not know the exact target model.

Chapter 6: Defense Strategies

6.1 Introduction to Defense Strategies

Defense strategies aim to protect machine learning models from adversarial attacks by either making the models more robust or detecting and mitigating the effects of the attacks. This chapter will explore various defense strategies that can be employed against FGSM and PGD attacks.

6.2 Adversarial Training

Adversarial training is a defense method that involves augmenting the training data with adversarial examples generated using methods such as FGSM or PGD. By exposing the model to adversarial examples during training, the model learns to be more robust against such attacks.

To implement adversarial training, the following steps can be taken:

Generate adversarial examples using FGSM or PGD for the current model.
Mix the adversarial examples with the original training data.
Retrain the model using the mixed dataset.
Adversarial training can significantly improve the model's robustness against adversarial attacks. However, it can also increase the training time and may not be effective against all types of attacks.

6.3 Defensive Distillation

Defensive distillation is a technique that trains a model (student) to mimic the output of another pre-trained model (teacher) while suppressing the gradient information that can be exploited by adversaries. The idea is to train the student model using the soft labels (probabilities) produced by the teacher model, which reduces the sensitivity of the student model to small input perturbations.

Steps for defensive distillation are as follows:

Train a teacher model using the original dataset.
Use the teacher model to generate soft labels for the training data.
Train the student model using the soft labels.
Defensive distillation can improve the model's robustness against FGSM and PGD attacks. However, it may not provide complete protection against more sophisticated attacks.

6.4 Gradient Masking and Input Transformations

Gradient masking is a defense technique that involves modifying the model's architecture or input data to make it difficult for adversaries to compute meaningful gradients. This can be achieved by introducing non-differentiable operations, such as quantization or binarization, into the model.

Input transformations are another approach to defend against adversarial attacks. By applying transformations like image resizing, random cropping, or noise addition to the input data, the adversarial perturbations can be disrupted, making it more difficult for the attack to succeed. However, these methods may not always provide robust defense and can sometimes be circumvented by adaptive adversaries.

6.5 Certification and Verification Methods

Certification and verification methods aim to provide guarantees on the model's robustness against adversarial attacks within a specified perturbation bound. These methods typically rely on mathematical techniques, such as convex optimization, to compute a certificate for each input, indicating the model's robustness to adversarial perturbations. Although these methods can provide strong theoretical guarantees, they can be computationally expensive and may not scale well to large, complex models.

Chapter 7: Real-World Applications and Future Directions

7.1 Security Implications of Adversarial Attacks

Adversarial attacks pose significant security challenges for various applications of machine learning, particularly in areas where model integrity is crucial, such as autonomous vehicles, facial recognition systems, and cybersecurity. For example, adversarial attacks could mislead an autonomous vehicle's perception system, causing it to misinterpret traffic signs or other objects, which could lead to accidents. Similarly, adversaries could exploit facial recognition systems to bypass security measures or create false identities.

7.2 Privacy Considerations in Adversarial Settings

In addition to security concerns, adversarial attacks can also have implications for privacy. Adversarial examples can be used to infer sensitive information about the training data or the model's internal workings, potentially revealing private details about the individuals or organizations involved. Developing robust defenses against these attacks is essential to protect user privacy and comply with data protection regulations.

7.3 Adversarial Attacks in Non-Image Domains

While much of the research on adversarial attacks has focused on image classification tasks, these attacks can also be applied to other domains such as natural language processing, speech recognition, and time-series analysis. In these domains, the input perturbations might be more subtle and difficult to detect, making the development of effective defense mechanisms even more crucial.

7.4 Future Research Directions

As machine learning models continue to be integrated into a wide range of applications, it is essential to develop more effective and efficient defenses against adversarial attacks. Some promising research directions include:

Developing more robust defense methods that can withstand adaptive and diverse attack strategies.
Investigating the transferability of adversarial examples across different models and domains to understand the underlying vulnerability patterns.
Studying the impact of adversarial attacks on reinforcement learning and generative models.
Exploring the use of techniques from cryptography, secure multiparty computation, and differential privacy to improve the robustness and privacy of machine learning models against adversarial attacks.

Chapter 8: Conclusion

This book has provided an in-depth exploration of adversarial attacks, focusing on the Fast Gradient Sign Method (FGSM) and Projected Gradient

Descent (PGD). We have discussed the motivations and applications of adversarial attacks, as well as the various defense strategies that can be employed to protect machine learning models from these attacks.

As machine learning continues to advance and become more pervasive in our daily lives, understanding and mitigating the risks posed by adversarial attacks is critical. By staying informed about the latest research and best practices in adversarial machine learning, practitioners can develop more robust and secure models that are better equipped to withstand the challenges posed by adversarial environments.

Chapter 9: Examples

Fast Gradient Sign Method (FGSM) and Projected Gradient Descent (PGD) are two popular adversarial attack methods. Here are Python code examples for both attacks using the TensorFlow library.

```python
import numpy as np
import tensorflow as tf
from tensorflow.keras.datasets import mnist
from tensorflow.keras.models import Sequential
from tensorflow.keras.layers import Dense, Flatten
from tensorflow.keras.utils import to_categorical

# Load and preprocess MNIST dataset
(x_train, y_train), (x_test, y_test) = mnist.load_data()
x_train, x_test = x_train / 255.0, x_test / 255.0
y_train, y_test = to_categorical(y_train), to_categorical(y_test)

# Build a simple model for MNIST classification
model = Sequential([
Flatten(input_shape=(28, 28)),
Dense(128, activation='relu'),
Dense(10, activation='softmax')
])

model.compile(optimizer='adam',
loss='categorical_crossentropy',
metrics=['accuracy'])

# Train the model
```

```python
model.fit(x_train, y_train, epochs=5)

# Evaluate the model
model.evaluate(x_test, y_test)
```

FGSM Attack:

```python
def fgsm_attack(                          ):
    sign_gradient = tf.sign(gradient)
    perturbed_image = image + epsilon * sign_gradient
    perturbed_image = tf.clip_by_value(perturbed_image, 0, 1)
    return perturbed_image

# Select a test image
image = tf.convert_to_tensor(x_test[0:1])

# Compute gradients for the image
with tf.GradientTape() as tape:
    tape.watch(image)
    prediction = model(image)
    loss = tf.keras.losses.categorical_crossentropy(y_test[0:1], prediction)

gradient = tape.gradient(loss, image)

# FGSM attack with epsilon = 0.1
epsilon = 0.1
perturbed_image = fgsm_attack(image, epsilon, gradient)
```

PGD Attack:

```python
def pgd_attack(                                              ):
    perturbed_image = image

    for _ in range(num_iterations):
        with tf.GradientTape() as tape:
            tape.watch(perturbed_image)
            prediction = model(perturbed_image)
            loss = tf.keras.losses.categorical_crossentropy(label, prediction)
```

```python
gradient = tape.gradient(loss, perturbed_image)
sign_gradient = tf.sign(gradient)
perturbed_image = perturbed_image + alpha * sign_gradient
perturbed_image = tf.clip_by_value(perturbed_image, image - epsilon, image
+ epsilon)
perturbed_image = tf.clip_by_value(perturbed_image, 0, 1)

return perturbed_image

# PGD attack with epsilon = 0.1, alpha = 0.01, and 40 iterations
epsilon = 0.1
alpha = 0.01
num_iterations = 40
perturbed_image = pgd_attack(model, image, y_test[0:1], epsilon, alpha,
num_iterations)
```

Here are some examples of FGSM and PGD attacks using the PyTorch library.

First, let's set up the environment and import the required libraries:

```python
import torch
import torch.nn as nn
import torch.optim as optim
import torchvision.transforms as transforms
from torchvision.datasets import MNIST
from torch.utils.data import DataLoader
from torchvision.models import resnet18
```

```python
# Check for GPU availability
device = torch.device("cuda:0" if torch.cuda.is_available() else "cpu")
```

```python
# Load and preprocess MNIST dataset
transform = transforms.Compose([transforms.Resize((224, 224)),
transforms.ToTensor()])
train_data = MNIST(root='./data', train=True, download=True,
transform=transform)
```

```python
test_data = MNIST(root='./data', train=False, download=True,
transform=transform)
train_loader = DataLoader(train_data, batch_size=32, shuffle=True)
test_loader = DataLoader(test_data, batch_size=1, shuffle=False)
```

Next, let's create and train a simple ResNet18 model for MNIST classification:

```python
# Build the ResNet18 model
model = resnet18(num_classes=10).to(device)
criterion = nn.CrossEntropyLoss()
optimizer = optim.Adam(model.parameters(), lr=0.001)
```

```python
# Train the model
for epoch in range(5):
    for images, labels in train_loader:
        images, labels = images.to(device), labels.to(device)
        optimizer.zero_grad()
        outputs = model(images)
        loss = criterion(outputs, labels)
        loss.backward()
        optimizer.step()
```

FGSM Attack:

```python
def fgsm_attack(                        ):
    sign_gradient = gradient.sign()
    perturbed_image = image + epsilon * sign_gradient
    perturbed_image = torch.clamp(perturbed_image, 0, 1)
    return perturbed_image
```

```python
# Select a test image
image, label = next(iter(test_loader))
image, label = image.to(device), label.to(device)
```

```python
# Compute gradients for the image
image.requires_grad = True
outputs = model(image)
loss = criterion(outputs, label)
```

```python
# Backpropagate the gradients
model.zero_grad()
loss.backward()
gradient = image.grad.data

# FGSM attack with epsilon = 0.1
epsilon = 0.1
perturbed_image = fgsm_attack(image, epsilon, gradient)
```

PGD Attack:

```python
def pgd_attack(                                                          ):
    perturbed_image = image.clone().detach()

    for _ in range(num_iterations):
        perturbed_image.requires_grad = True
        outputs = model(perturbed_image)
        loss = criterion(outputs, label)

        model.zero_grad()
        loss.backward()
        gradient = perturbed_image.grad.data

        sign_gradient = gradient.sign()
        perturbed_image = perturbed_image + alpha * sign_gradient
        perturbation = torch.clamp(perturbed_image - image, -epsilon, epsilon)
        perturbed_image = torch.clamp(image + perturbation, 0, 1).detach()

    return perturbed_image

# PGD attack with epsilon = 0.1, alpha = 0.01, and 40 iterations
epsilon = 0.1
alpha = 0.01
num_iterations = 40
perturbed_image = pgd_attack(model, image, label, epsilon, alpha,
num_iterations)
```

These code examples demonstrate how to perform FGSM and PGD attacks on a simple ResNet18 model for MNIST classification using PyTorch. In both examples, we first compute the gradients of the loss with respect to the input image and then use these gradients to generate adversarial examples

Synopsis

This book offers a comprehensive examination of adversarial attacks in machine learning, with a focus on the Fast Gradient Sign Method (FGSM) and Projected Gradient Descent (PGD) techniques. The text begins with an introduction to adversarial machine learning and the concept of adversarial examples, providing context for the motivations and applications of these attacks. The book then delves into the FGSM and PGD techniques, detailing their algorithms, formulations, and various attack variants. A comparative analysis of FGSM and PGD is provided, highlighting their strengths, weaknesses, and the transferability of adversarial examples. To counteract adversarial attacks, the book explores several defense strategies, including adversarial training, defensive distillation, gradient masking, input transformations, and certification and verification methods. Real-world applications of adversarial attacks are discussed, along with their security and privacy implications. Finally, the book outlines future research directions in adversarial machine learning, underscoring the importance of understanding and mitigating adversarial attacks as machine learning models become more pervasive in everyday life. By staying informed about the latest research and best practices, practitioners can develop more robust and secure models capable of withstanding adversarial challenges.

Ethics

Ethical practices are paramount when working with adversarial attacks and defenses in artificial intelligence (AI). Here's a more detailed overview of these ethical considerations:

Responsible AI Development: Ethical practitioners prioritize the responsible development of AI systems. This involves creating AI models that are not only effective but also robust, transparent, and fair. Responsible AI development ensures that AI technology is used for the benefit of society.

Transparency: Transparency is a fundamental aspect of ethical AI. Practitioners strive to be transparent about potential vulnerabilities to adversarial attacks and the steps taken to defend against them. Transparency builds trust and accountability in AI development.

Data Privacy: Protecting user data and privacy is a core ethical principle. Adhering to data privacy regulations and best practices when collecting, storing, and processing data is crucial. Ethical practitioners ensure that data is handled responsibly and securely.

Bias Mitigation: Ethical AI practitioners actively work to identify and mitigate biases in machine learning models. This includes efforts to ensure that AI systems do not discriminate against specific groups and do not perpetuate harmful biases.

Ethical Use: Ethical practitioners commit to using AI technology for ethical purposes. They do not engage in malicious or harmful activities using adversarial attacks. Responsible use of AI is a key ethical consideration.

Public Awareness: Ethical AI practitioners contribute to public awareness about adversarial attacks. This includes educating the public, policymakers, and stakeholders about the risks and defenses associated with AI systems. Public awareness promotes informed discussions and decisions about AI technology.

Continuous Monitoring and Improvement: Ethical AI development is an ongoing process. Practitioners continuously monitor AI models for vulnerabilities and adapt defenses as new threats emerge. This iterative approach ensures the ongoing security and reliability of AI systems.

Collaboration: Collaboration within the AI community is vital. Ethical practitioners work together to share knowledge and best practices for defending against adversarial attacks. Collaboration strengthens the AI field and its ability to address threats effectively.

Regulation and Compliance: Ethical AI practitioners adhere to ethical and legal frameworks and regulations. They are aware of and comply with laws and regulations related to data privacy, security, and AI development. Compliance ensures ethical boundaries are maintained.

Ethical Research: Researchers conduct ethical research and avoid using adversarial attacks to harm or exploit AI systems. Ethical research contributes positively to the advancement of AI technology for the benefit of society.

In essence, ethical practices in working with adversarial attacks and defenses encompass responsible development, transparency, data privacy, bias mitigation, ethical use, public awareness, continuous monitoring, collaboration, compliance with regulations, and ethical research. These practices collectively contribute to the ethical advancement of AI technology, ensuring its trustworthiness and responsible use in society.

Additional Reading Pt. 1

"Adversarial Machine Learning" by Anthony D. Joseph, Blaine Nelson, Benjamin I.P. Rubinstein, and J.D. Tygar
This book provides an in-depth exploration of adversarial machine learning, covering a wide range of attack and defense techniques. It offers insights into the challenges posed by adversarial attacks and strategies to build robust machine learning models.

"Deep Learning" by Ian Goodfellow, Yoshua Bengio, and Aaron Courville
Chapter 7 of this foundational book on deep learning is dedicated to
adversarial training and adversarial examples. It provides a comprehensive
introduction to the topic and offers a deeper understanding of adversarial
attacks and defenses.

"Explaining Machine Learning: An Overlooked Challenge" by Christoph
Molnar
Understanding model behavior is crucial for robustness. This book chapter
provides insights into model interpretability and the challenges of adversarial
examples, shedding light on the importance of explainable AI.

"Robustness and Security of Deep Learning" by Shuiwang Ji, Wah Chiu, and
Shuicheng Yan
This comprehensive survey paper covers various aspects of adversarial
attacks and defenses in deep learning. It offers an overview of the state-of-
the-art techniques and the latest research in the field.

"Adversarial Attacks and Defenses in Deep Learning" by Luiz H. G. Ceschin,
Gustavo Carneiro, and Andrew P. King
This book chapter provides insights into adversarial attacks and defenses in
medical image analysis, a critical domain where AI systems must be robust
and reliable.

Additional Reading Pt. 2

"Towards Evaluating the Robustness of Neural Networks" by Nicholas Carlini and David A. Wagner
This influential paper introduces various techniques for generating adversarial examples and discusses the challenges in evaluating the robustness of neural networks.

"The Clever Hans Phenomenon: A Survey" by Gary Marcus
This survey paper explores the broader context of the Clever Hans phenomenon, shedding light on issues related to machine learning interpretability and adversarial attacks.

"Adversarial Attacks and Defenses: A Survey" by Muhammad Usama, Asim Mehmood, and Zohaib Anwar
This survey provides a comprehensive overview of adversarial attacks and defenses, including recent developments and emerging trends in the field.

"Interpretable Machine Learning" by Christoph Molnar
Understanding machine learning models is crucial for identifying vulnerabilities and developing effective defenses against adversarial attacks. This book focuses on model interpretability and transparency.

"Machine Learning Yearning" by Andrew Ng
This practical guidebook by AI pioneer Andrew Ng includes a chapter on AI system design and the importance of identifying and mitigating risks, including adversarial attacks, in real-world AI applications.

www.ingramcontent.com/pod-product-compliance
Lightning Source LLC
LaVergne TN
LVHW022126060326
832903LV00063B/4790